SKI in a day!

Akira Honda
4712 So. Morgan St.
Seattle, Wa.   98118

PHOTOGRAPHS BY **KIM MASSIE**

SKI in a day!

CLIF TAYLOR

CERTIFIED SKI INSTRUCTOR

GROSSET & DUNLAP
Publishers   NEW YORK

This is a skier's book by skiers. My thanks to journalist and expert skier Mort Lund, who has followed my short-ski method since its inception, for his help in the writing of this book; to ski photographer Kim Massie for his excellent pictures; to my adroit pupil Sandra Heath for helping me demonstrate short-ski teaching; to twins Sally & Sue White; to Hogback Ski Area, Vermont, for providing the snow; and to editor Conrad Brown, long-time friend and ski professional, for advice.

C.T.

To my friend and fellow skier,
LOWELL THOMAS, whose enthusiastic support
for my short-ski method has been
an inspiration to me.

THE FUN OF SKIING CAN CHANGE
YOUR WHOLE OUTLOOK ON WINTER

CONTENTS

YOU REALLY CAN SKI IN A DAY

Ever since I became an instructor I have been seeking a way to get my students skiing in less time with less effort. The method I evolved proves to be the quickest and easiest approach by far to safe, controlled skiing — and thousands have learned to ski my new SKI IN A DAY way.

The combination of very short skis and simple step-by-step method for learning to use them eliminates tedious hours of difficult maneuvers demanded of those who begin on long skis.

My many years of ski teaching convince me that all skiers, regardless of age, should start on very short skis. The shortest ones (2 ½ feet long) are perfect for the packed slopes that all beginners learn on. Medium short skis (four feet long) are excellent all-around skis for recreational skiing, good on any steepness of slope or trail under absolutely all snow conditions, even deep powdery snow.

On short skis you learn with the least expenditure of effort and develop a smooth, graceful technique that can be applied to long skis once you have become used to the idea of sliding down a snow-covered mountainside.

As you take up skiing, a single admonition: don't become so serious about your progress that you exclude the fun from the sport. It's not work, it's easy to learn to ski.

Come ski with me and see. You can be a skier in a day!

CLIF TAYLOR

CHAPTER 1

THE SHORT-SKI WAY: FAST ROAD TO SKIING

There are two approaches to this sport. One is the traditional long-ski route that starts you in the awkward and strenuous "snowplow" (see facing page) and takes you through various stages calling for opening and closing the skis, until you finally reach the goal of "parallel" skiing, feet together.

The new approach, the short-ski way that this book teaches, is gaining ground in ski schools all across the country. It starts you skiing parallel on very short skis, graduates you to slightly longer skis as you gain proficiency, and finally puts you on skis as long as you can handle.

By keeping the technique the same throughout, the snowplow is eliminated. This means you can begin skiing a comfortable skis-together style right away, instead of spending years conquering the snowplow and the snowplow-type turns, and then having to unlearn them for the easier parallel turns.

Onward then to short-ski parallel skiing!

THE SHORT-SKI WAY: BEGINNER STARTS PARALLEL. . . .

SAME PARALLEL TECHNIQUE TRANSFERS TO LONG SKIS

THE LONG-SKI WAY: BEGINNER STARTS SNOWPLOW . . .

PROGRESSES LATER TO PARALLEL TECHNIQUE

HOW YOU SLOW DOWN

. . . or you can make turns all the way down the hill.
This is much more like it! Each turn slows you
a bit and you come down the slope under control.

TURNING MEANS CONTROL

Turning "puts on the brakes." The whole concept of modern skiing is based on controlling your downhill flight by turning.

Turns control the effect of gravity: gravity speeds you up, turning your skis slows you down.

The dangerous skier is the one who cannot turn. Don't point your skis straight downhill until you have learned to control your speed by turning them. Your next step is learning the secret of turning.

CHAPTER 2

THE SECRET OF TURNING

There is no secret, really. You merely turn the feet in a new direction and the skis turn with them. It is as simple as that, in spite of the many different theories you may have heard on what makes a ski turn.

There are various sorts of turns, but the basic modern kind — the turn on which good skiers depend — is the one in which the muscles of the body turn the feet and the feet turn the skis. This is the parallel turn. You can learn parallel in one day on short skis. If you use long skis it will take much longer.

HOW TO LEARN TURNING

You don't need snow or skis to practice proper parallel turning technique: Simply stand up straight on a small scatter rug on a polished floor. Flex your knees, feet flat, weight balanced mostly on the ball of each foot. Now hold your arms out at the sides and turn both feet abruptly to the left, then abruptly to the right. Keep your upper body facing straight ahead as you twist the rug continuously left and right.

TWIST LEFT

If you twist your feet with the same rhythmic motion when you're on skis gliding down a slope, you'll get the nice curved track you see on the facing page.

If you haven't got a scatter rug handy, practice without one, turning both feet back and forth in the same direction at the same time.

Do the twist until you can make 10 consecutive turns without stopping. This develops your reflexes, timing, and rhythm.

TWIST RIGHT

START

TWIST RIGHT

HOW TO TURN YOUR SKIS: THE SHORT-SKI TWIST

Turning your skis on snow is as easy as turning your feet on a rug. Find a nice smooth hard-packed place. Stamp the snow flat with your skis if it's too soft.

STAND —

- body erect balanced over the balls of the feet
- boots together, knees flexed
- weight evenly distributed on both skis
- arms out

NOW —

- twist the skis clockwise and counterclockwise in a continuous rhythmic motion, left-right-left-right
- keep the upper body facing straight ahead
- let the arms swing freely for balance

If the skis don't twist easily, your weight may be too far forward or more likely too far back. Check to see if your skis are fanning the snow equally in front and in back, making the symmetrical hourglass pattern you see in the snow in these pictures. A perfect "hourglass" means that you are twisting correctly on the balls of your feet.

Twisting in place on shortees is a vital preliminary to turning on the hill. Keep at it until you can do it easily ten consecutive times.

TWIST LEFT

HOW TO TWIST DOWN THE SLOPE

Once you have learned to twist in place, the next step is to pick a smooth, easy slope and start down it at slow speed. As you move, begin twisting the same way you twisted on the rug and on your skis in place. Don't go very far before making your first

TWIST . . .

HOW TO MAKE
10 PARALLEL TURNS
DOWNHILL

Don't make just one turn. Continue twisting left and right until you have completed 10 linked turns. Your skis will trace the graceful, swivel pattern in the snow that spells moderate speed and good control.

Pick a slope with nothing in your way, so that you can make your turns rhythmically. Make it a dance motion — gentle, light-footed and easy, with a curving glide between each twist.

You will find that you can make a turn anytime. And since you are making turns all the time, you never get going so fast that you have any trouble avoiding obstacles that may get in front of you.

Continuous turning controls your speed and makes you sure-footed on the ski slope. Practice 10 short turns, and then 10 longer ones.

A tip: If you feel yourself losing your balance in a turn, quickly twist in the opposite direction. This will keep you from falling.

HOW TO MAKE SHORT TURNS
AND LONG ONES

There are two types of ski turn in the short-ski technique. First, there are short turns, such as those on this page, which come from fast back-and-forth twisting. This controls your speed very efficiently. Then there are the long turns (see facing page) which allow you more speed. They are more fun although they take more room on the slope.

You will have to be the judge of whether the slope is free of obstacles, but if you want to make long turns, you will find that you can make them simply by gliding longer during and after each twist.

The track on the facing page represents the distance traveled during one twist, while the track on this page represents a distance traveled while many twist turns were being done.

Quick twists mean tight control. Long gliding twists mean speed and an exciting swooping sensation.

SHORT TURNS

LONG TURN

HOW TO CLIMB HERRINGBONE STYLE

Up to now you have been keeping your skis fairly flat. To climb back up for another run down, you will have to make the skis bite into the snow.

(Avoid riding a ski lift during the first few hours on shortees. Lift riding comes after you have gained confidence in your ability to turn. Climb up and ski down a a few times.)

To go up, as demonstrated on this page, the inside edges of the skis must grip the snow with each step upward. The skis themselves cannot be pointed straight up the hill or they would slip backward. Instead, point them out.

Keeping your knees flexed, make each step a forthright slam of the ski in the snow, so that the inside edge bites and holds.

This is called the herringbone, and it's a lot easier on shortees than it is on long skis.

HOW TO CLIMB SIDE-STEP STYLE

You may want to vary your manner of climbing the hill, and side-stepping is a second uphill method available to you.

Simply step the skis up sideways, with the uphill edge of the ski biting into the snow, almost as if you were stepping a little series of ledges, one step to each ledge.

This is the way you'd walk up a very steep embankment in your shoes. Side-stepping on skis is not much different, provided you make a definite stamping motion to set the uphill edge of the ski firmly in the snow.

MOVE ACROSS THE SLOPE...

...UNTIL YOU STOP

HOW TO STOP

The art of stopping in skiing is simply the act of turning until you are moving directly across the slope: friction will soon slow you to a stop. This is traversing to a stop.

HOW TO ZIGZAG BACK UP

Sometimes it is easier to zigzag back up a slope, particularly after you have run down it quite a few times, rather than to herringbone or side-step up. When you zigzag, you are <u>traversing upward</u> on a ski slope.

CHAPTER 3

RHYTHM BRINGS POWER AND BALANCE

Now you have skied downhill, and learned how to climb back up. The next stage is rhythm. On short skis it is part of the early phase of learning.

Real control over your skis and your rate of descent comes when you can deliberately mix your turns, short and long. The best way to start is to think of the cha-cha dance rhythm and do two long turns, followed immediately by three short ones: one, two . . . one, two, three. And again: one, two . . . one, two, three.

Practice this and you'll soon be able to make long-radius turns or quick, short ones at will. The more consciously you ski with rhythm the more stable you'll become on your skis.

Keep your arms out for balance.

Stand with your weight right over the skis, not behind them or ahead of them. Go with them, don't hang back. YOU have control now.

After a few tries at this cha-cha beat, you'll be skiing with the rhythm that distinguishes the advanced skier from the beginner.

FOUR-FOOT SKIS
IN POWDER SNOW

RHYTHM-TURNS

It is important in acquiring rhythm that you think of making turns in series all the way to the bottom of the slope. A good skier sails from one turn to the next down the hill. The reason for this is that swinging from one turn to another gives him the equilibrium engineers call "dynamic stability," the stability that comes of being in a constant cycle of motion.

So swing from one turn to another. As soon as a turn is finished begin the next, don't wait. To build up confidence, make ten consecutive turns without stopping.

Rhythm is important for another reason: its essence in skiing is having a good time. If you are not having fun while you are learning, you can't really swing into rhythm turns. And with short skis there is no excuse for not having fun.

JUMP AROUND!

Get as much variety into each day as possible. Here is an exercise in facing the skis about that will liven your day and loosen you up for more practice at twist turns. Jump your skis around. It's easy with short skis. And it will keep you from getting too tense.

HOW TO: FOOT-TURN

LEG-TURN

HIP-TURN TO GET RHYTHM AND CONTROL

So far you have been turning more or less without thought of just how you were twisting, but there are various types of twist turn.

First, as shown on the facing page, there is the foot-turn. Here you twist (rotate) mostly at the ankles, the tips of the skis just making a little wiggle back and forth in front of you as you move down the hill. (Go back to the scatter rug again and try twisting at the ankles alone.)

Next comes the leg-turn, in which the legs rotate at the thigh joints. Turn the page and you will see that this develops a greater back-and-forth movement of the tips and wider arcs across the hill. (Try the leg-turn on your rug too.) Leg-turns give a skier more stopping power than foot-turns.

Finally there is the hip-turn, and here the whole hip is rotated to get the skis turning; the major twisting of the body is at the waist. (The shoulders continue to face the general direction of the skier's descent as the lower body rotates in the turns.) Hip-turns make still wider arcs, as you'll see on the following pages, and give the greatest stopping and slowing-down power of all.

It is important to teach yourself the various ways of twisting — with the feet; with the legs; with the whole lower body — so you can use all the twisting muscles you have and gain control in your skiing. It is important to vary the kinds of turns you do as you ski in order to acquire precision in your skiing. Practice sets of turns, mixing short ones and long ones using any combination you like. Making one kind of turn all the way down the slope leads to monotony. It's more fun to learn various kinds of turns and mix them up.

FOOT-TURNS

LEG-TURNS

Leg-turns are larger, stronger and more pronounced than foot-turns, because the legs twist the skis farther.

HIP-TURNS

Hip-turns are the largest and strongest of all. They give you the greatest amount of braking action. You really <u>twist</u> those skis when you rotate your lower body from the waist.

DANCE DOWN THE SLOPE

On the facing page: a particularly enjoyable set of eight consecutive turns on four-foot shortees. Look closely at the way the skis are planing in the new powder snow. A ski this length is fun in deep snow because it turns so easily.

The whole concept of rhythm in skiing is made clear: what you want is something that gets you going and makes you want to keep going from curve to curve and swing to swing. This is the essence of having fun in recreational skiing (and is the key to good racing as well).

The key is rhythm.

MIX SHORT TURNS WITH LONG TURNS

THE MECHANISM

What makes those skis turn?

It's a question that begets an argument wherever skiers gather. There are various forces that can make a ski turn, and for the sake of those who do better when they know what the principles are, here is a short explanation of the turning force.

It is, of course, the twist that does it: a scientist would say that you are employing an action-reaction force. All this means is that a given rotation in one part of the body generates an opposite rotation in another part of the body. Thus if you swing the lower body (and skis) in one direction, the upper body automatically counter-rotates in the other direction without conscious effort.

This type of turn is the so-called "reverse" turn discovered and refined by racers early in the past decade. The reverse turn was subsequently applied to recreational skiing at the advanced or parallel level. Now short skis make it possible to use this powerful turn at the beginning level — your first day on skis.

The sequence on the facing page shows this: the counterclockwise rotation of arms and upper body is a direct result of a clockwise rotation of the lower body and ankles.

This is the mechanism in swinging a turn.

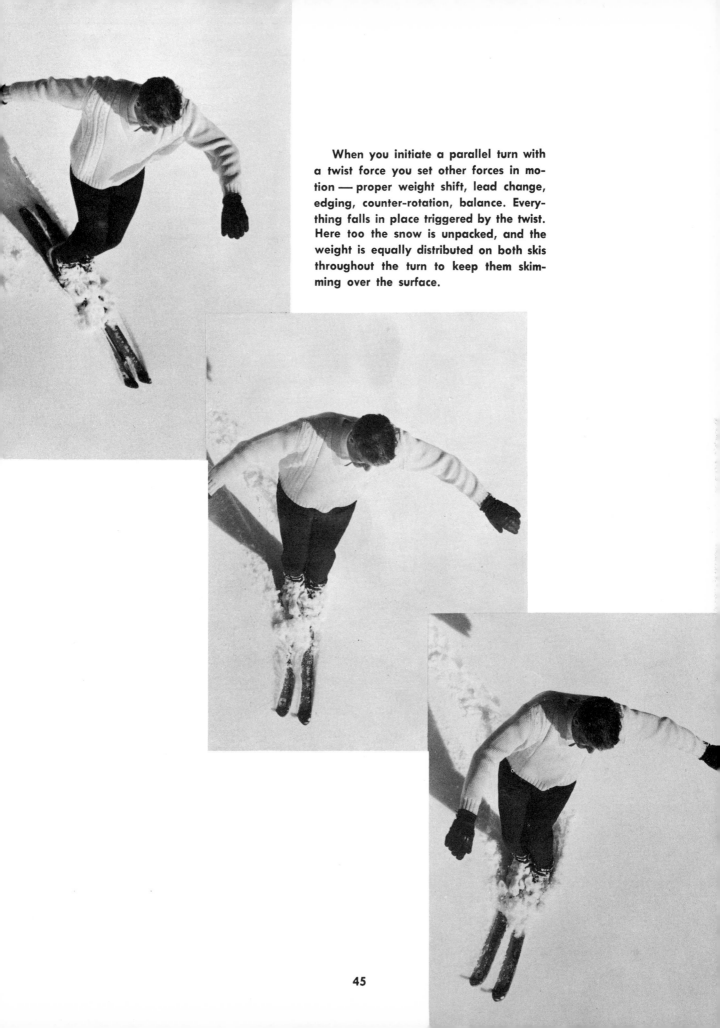

When you initiate a parallel turn with a twist force you set other forces in motion — proper weight shift, lead change, edging, counter-rotation, balance. Everything falls in place triggered by the twist. Here too the snow is unpacked, and the weight is equally distributed on both skis throughout the turn to keep them skimming over the surface.

CHAPTER 4

THE THEORY AND PRACTICE
OF ENJOYING SKIING

Enjoying your skiing is the ultimate goal. It is not something apart from improving your technique. There is no such thing as learning to ski while hating skiing and then hoping you will enjoy the sport later on. You should enjoy your skiing as you learn, and that means getting as much variety into your ski day as possible, doing some things just for kicks.

A pair of young ladies — twins — demonstrate this attitude. They are on short skis, as you can see, 2½-footers. Both girls love to experiment with new stunts. These may not fit into any specific pattern of learning but they help them enjoy their day on skis, improving their technique.

THE FUN OF FALLING

One of the things that makes the twins good skiers is that they don't mind falling, and why should they? Short skis make falling almost a pleasure. It is axiomatic in this sport anyway that when you stop falling you stop learning. Sure, our twin is disappointed at not being able to hold one ski in the air indefinitely, but the fall is nothing. If you put too much stress on staying upright you will turn into a rigid skier instead of a graceful one.

So don't be afraid to let yourself go. Pick yourself up, brush yourself off and start all over again.

Here the twins are playing "train." They actually ski this way sometimes just as a stunt.

HOW TO SKI ON ONE SKI

JUMPING IS FUN

For the more athletically inclined, here is a soaring jump-up between a pair of ski poles that is fun to do. (Later on you'll be shown how the poles are used in downhill skiing.) The whole idea of the pole jump is to get as far off the ground as possible and come down as lightly as a bird landing on a branch.

If you want to make this into a jump-turn, simply turn the skis in a new direction as you come down.

TEACHER AND PUPIL BEGIN

CHAPTER 5

HOW TO GIVE A PRIVATE LESSON

Everyone who learns to ski finds he would like to pass some of his fun along to others, particularly to members of his family. Here's the way the short-ski method is taught in the ski schools across the country that have adopted the method. The short-ski teacher can take on groups or, as shown here, give a "private" lesson. The method is the same as learning by yourself—the subject of this book to this point. The difference is that instead of looking at pictures, the pupil watches the teacher.

The first step, twisting on a scatter rug, we will not show here, but the student has practiced it in the ski lodge. The second step, turning the skis in place in the snow, is the same: teacher and pupil keep time together as they twist. Left-right-left-right. Make sure the snow is packed under the skis before beginning.

The teacher in the short-ski method should be responsible for seeing that learning is fun. No shouting, no scolding — please.

When the pupil can twist left and right 10 consecutive times with easy rhythm, the pupil is ready to try a small hill with a flat runout.

TWIST ONE WAY

TWIST THE OTHER

THE SIMPLEST WAY TO TEACH

TEACHER AND PUPIL TWIST

. . . THE PUPIL GETS THE IDEA

TEACHER MAKES A TRACK...

...PUPIL FOLLOWS IT

...AND SKIS THE MOUNTAIN
THE SAME DAY

LESSON'S END

CELEBRITIES ON SHORTEES

Short skis are a godsend for the young — and the not-so-young. Adults haven't got the time, or the disposition, to go through the tedious process of re-learning how to ski each year on the long ones.

Starting late, my wife and I never did learn to make neat turns with our feet together — which we can do now on short skis. Thus we get far more pleasure from the limited time that we are able to devote to the sport. We enjoy our downhill skiing instead of being frustrated by our ineptitude.

One day's instruction and we were converted. My wife and I even skied holding hands after an hour or so on shortees.

COMMANDER EDWARD WHITEHEAD

CHAPTER **6**

FAMILY SKIING

The great thing about short skis is that you can get the youngest member of the family started, then use the same pair to teach the next oldest, and so on up the line. (There's a new binding on the market called the "Tiesler Zip Fit" that adjusts easily and instantly without tools to fit any size boot, and releases in a fall.)

Right at the outset a small child has got to be convinced that all this is a lot of fun. Let him walk around on his skis quite a while before persuading him to climb the hill with them. Then teach him how to walk uphill. If he wants to be carried, carry him up a little way. It's no problem; he's wearing short skis. If he wants to quit and chase indoors, let him go. He probably knows best, as Dr. Spock would say. Any hint of forcing him to ski will make him dislike the whole idea, and you may lose his interest in skiing for the rest of the winter. Get him to agree to each new thing you try.

HOW TO TEACH THE YOUNGEST

READY . . .

If he wants you to steady him, hold him up gently, but don't ski down with a young-ster as you might with an older pupil. It doesn't work, a child's movements are too unpredictable. It's better to let him go on his own and even fall, rather than try to hold him up when he's underway. He'll catch on and soon ski standing up.

Let a five year old on skis play as much as he wants. To get him skiing down play slopes, encourage him to follow you. You can teach him best just by letting him mimic you. Teach him simple twist turns, feet together, as soon as possible. If he gets in funny off-balance positions skiing down, merely suggest that he'll find it easier if he stands up straight.

One final word: don't worry — children hardly ever get hurt skiing.

. . . GO!

Our youngster, slowly moving down the hill under his own steam. A couple more runs and you won't be able to get those skis away from him. Short skis are just the ticket for the short skier.

ON SHORT SKIS IT'S PARALLEL TURNS

PAAR FOR THE COURSE

Here is a famous father who has never been on skis before. It's Jack Paar, come to Vermont to learn to ski in a day.

Jack and his daughter Randy learn the twist in place, their short skis making the required little hourglass patterns in the snow.

SKI WE DID

It was Lowell Thomas who got me interested in the new Taylor method. I don't have time to spend years learning a sport, so the instant-skiing idea appealed to me immediately. It sounded like a great way to get my family started in this popular winter recreation.

So away we went to find Clif Taylor. We really did learn to ski in a day.

He took us out on shortee skis to a flat place on the snow and told us to twist — just like the dance — turning our shortees left and right while standing in one place.

A few minutes later we were skiing the novice slope doing the same twist going downhill. I caught on as quickly as my daughter Randy.

By afternoon we were riding up the lift and Clif had us skiing the big slopes, in control, making lots of turns.

I felt like an instructor; I asked for an armband.

For our second lesson, Clif put us on four-foot shortees. To our amazement, the longer skis were as easy as the shorter ones, only we went faster — still under control and using the same technique.

By the end of the day we had conquered the mountain.

Suddenly we were skiers!

JACK PAAR

Jack starts down from the top of the mountain
on four-footers at the end of his second lesson.

CHAPTER 7

ADVANCED SKIING

There are refinements and tricks to skiing that will make your skiing more precise, more controlled and enable you to start skiing faster as you become sure of your ability to go exactly where you want to go. These refinements come under the heading of weight-shift, banking, edging, lead change, skidding, pole use, backward-and-forward shifting, trail running and bump handling — all in this chapter. In this picture you see the kind of control you can get with these refinements. I am running through a set of slalom poles which are race course markers used in slalom racing. The idea is to come close to the inside pole of the gate as you go through it, and on to the next gate in the course.

HOW TO SHIFT WEIGHT

You have the choice of putting all your weight on both skis or on one ski in any turn. For more buoyancy on new snow, weight both skis equally throughout the turn. For better balance and grip on hard icy snow, start your turns on one ski and gradually weight both skis as you change direction. When you weight one ski more than the other, make it the outside ski of the turn that gets most of your weight.

HOW TO BANK AND EDGE

In modern skiing you bank the lower body toward the center of the turn to offset the force of momentum. The banking automatically rolls your skis on their edges, carving a smooth arc and gripping the snow. As your lower body banks, your upper body should stay more or less vertical for balance. With proper banking and edging you will make smooth sweeping turns like the one shown here.

HOW TO EDGE WITH THE KNEES

Banking the body tends to edge the skis, but more than that, edging requires that the sides of the knees press toward the hill. In this picture, notice how the bent knees pressed toward the slope make the edges of the skis bite into the snow. That's what you want. The bite keeps your skis from slipping sideways out from under you in a fast turn, especially when you are skiing hard-packed or icy snow.

If you look at the facing page you can see how the knee bend, together with the banking body, brings the skis up on edge sufficiently to allow a high-speed turn to be made with ease.

DOWN THE BIG SLOPES ON FOUR-FOOT SHORTEES AT ASPEN, COLORADO.
NOTICE HOW THE SHOULDERS STAY FACING DOWNHILL
AS THE HIPS, KNEES AND FEET TURN THE SKIS.

HOW TO CHANGE LEAD

The best way to keep your skis from crossing, particularly as you move up to longer skis, is to advance the inside ski of each turn about half a boot-length ahead of the outside ski. This leading with one ski then leading with the other is called "lead change." In the pictures you can clearly see that, as the skier moves from one turn to the next, the inside ski is always advanced.

HOW TO SKID

Sometimes, rather than banking or edging the ski so it will hold and not skid, you <u>want</u> the ski to skid. This is particularly true in turns where there isn't much outward pull on the body, as in the picture here. To make skis skid they are kept fairly flat on the snow.

You should try both edged turns and skid turns in practice so you'll know which you want at any given moment.

SEVEN-FOOT SKIS

HOW TO USE POLES

We have ignored ski poles up to this point because it is better to get acquainted with your skis first, and then your poles. When you are just beginning, ski poles get in your way.

But the greatest trouble with poles is that too many skiers tend to lean on them as they turn. It's better to learn without poles and you won't be tempted to develop a bad habit. Besides, lots of people who ski on short skis exclusively find it is just plain more enjoyable to ski without poles.

When you do start using them, hold them out from your body without putting the points in the snow as you ski down. When you've got used to skiing with them, practice just touching a pole in the snow at the beginning of each turn (as in the sequence above) for rhythm.

Used this way, the pole is a help in skiing. But don't let yourself lean on those poles. Every once in a while make a run without them to make sure your poles haven't become crutches for you.

Poles are handy for climbing, once you have learned to carry them with you down-hill without having them get in your way.

Use the leather strap correctly: Entire hand and thumb up through the strap from below the loop; then, strap firmly encircling the back of the wrist, hand grasps the pole with strap in the palm.

FOUR-FOOT SKIS
IN POWDER SNOW

HOW TO SHIFT WEIGHT FORWARD AND BACKWARD

As you progress in skiing, you will have to give some thought to the position of your weight over your skis. In general, the weight should center over your boots, with your body preferably at a right angle to the slope of your track, no matter how steep the hill. However, there will be times when you will need to bring the weight back a bit. Deep powder snow, when you must keep the tips of the skis up and planing (as above), is one of those times.

When the snow gets like ice, you must lean forward more to make the skis cut in better.

HOW TO SKI TRAILS

Running a trail is an art that demands instantaneous study of the constantly changing terrain before you. Be alert to the possibilities. For instance, you can make use of the steep banks along the sides of a trail for turning and reducing your speed.

Every trail has an easy way and a hard way down. Don't pick out the easy way and ski it over and over every run. Vary your descent and improve your skiing faster.

Notice in the picture above the skiers' natural skiing stance, knees and ankles flexed, ready to absorb the bumps as they glide over them.

HOW TO SKI BUMPS

The best way to handle the bumps that skiers call "moguls" is to ride off the sides and backs of them, using bumps as small banks and letting them help your turns. In the picture you can see I am riding off one to my left while the twins ride off a mogul to their right. If you can swing from the side of one mogul to the side of another, right on down the mountain, you will find you can maintain good safe speed and stay completely in control even on very steep trails.

HOW TO SKI A RUNOUT

The long flat stretches at the end of many ski trails are called "runouts." They are often slow and boring. Here is one way to handle them. Get down into the racing "egg" position and tuck the poles up under your arms. The legs can be more separated than usual for stability. The egg position keeps your weight somewhat on the back of your skis, which makes them run faster. And the low position cuts down wind resistance.

HOW TO SKATE ON SKIS

Skating is a good way to improve your balance and feeling for snow. The principle is much the same as skating on ice. Just step off at an angle to the left on the left ski and glide. Then step off at an angle on the right ski — and keep going! You have to make a fast and powerful movement onto each new ski as you skate onto it, the way a speed skater lunges forward with his weight at each new step. Skating is particularly useful on flatter slopes like runouts.

Try to feel the fun of it. That will do more to make you skate well than anything else.

HOW TO DO A REUEL

The reuel (pronounced "royal") is a variation of the skating step in which you glide longer and hold the lifted ski out and somewhat back as you make a turn on the ski that remains on the snow. It's a turn totally on the inside ski (remember in an orthodox two-ski turn your weight is mostly on the outside ski of the turn).

To make a reuel you have to keep the body leaning to the inside of the turn. It's a fun turn that helps develop your balance.

ALL THREE LENGTHS OF SHORTEE SKI ARE FINE FOR RECREATIONAL SKIING — 2½-FOOTERS FOR INSTANT PARALLEL TECHNIQUE AND FUN ON HARD PACKED SNOW; FOUR-FOOTERS FOR EASY SKIING ON ALL TYPES OF SNOW; FIVE-FOOTERS FOR MORE SPEED. SHORT SKIS DIFFER FROM LONG SKIS ONLY IN LENGTH AND TAPER AND SHOULD BE NO WIDER THAN LONG SKIS. ANYTHING WIDER IS HARD TO CONTROL.

CHAPTER **8**

SHORTS TO LONGS

In the final analysis, the function of short skis is to give you a chance to work up to the most suitable length of ski for the kind of skiing that suits you best. Short skis are excellent all-purpose recreational skis too.

The 2½-foot ski is the length we have been dealing with throughout most of the book. The next step up is the four-foot ski, above.

And this is the beauty of the short-ski method: the technique for going on to longer skis is the same as you have learned so far. As in the picture above, you merely take them out on the snow and twist in place before you try it downhill.

IT'S ONE AND...

...TWO AND...

...YOU'RE OFF!

HOW TO FIND
YOUR BEST LENGTH SKI

After you can ski the four-footers as well as you can ski the 2½-footers, you can go to longer skis easily. Try five-footers next. The technique is the same, except that after four-footers you start applying the added factor of lift: Just before you go into your turn you press your knees forward in a slight crouch. Then (keeping your body forward) bounce up to full height as you twist. This movement takes some of the weight off your skis and makes the turn easier to start because the friction under your skis is reduced. As you can see, the technique is otherwise the same on 2½-footers, fours, right up to seven-footers such as racers and experts use with ease.

Why go to long skis at all? Short skis can be compared to a sportscar — it will go anywhere a limousine will go but is much more maneuverable. Four-footers, for example, are much easier to handle than seven-foot skis in new powder snow and on big steep bumpy slopes.

Shortees are not as fast as long racing skis, but they are plenty fast enough for recreational skiing. Be forewarned that nothing is more discouraging than to get on long skis too soon and have to spend hours and days at the foot of the mountain on the beginners' slope getting used to them.

What's the best length for you? Answer: the length of ski you find easiest to handle on the trails you prefer to ski.

2½-FOOTERS

90

IN SUMMARY

Trail blazing is never easy. Millions who have learned to ski the long-ski route are going to continue arguing against short skis until they try the skis themselves or see someone close to them learn on short skis — miraculously — in hours. A new learning method is only as good as its results. Hear what Pan American Airways Captain M. LODEESEN has to say:

"Having been an occasional weekend skier, I gave up the sport ten years ago as being too dangerous for a man of 59 with my responsibilities . . . I had never gotten beyond simple stem turns, never felt secure except on gentle slopes.

"This fall I read about your short-ski system and instantly knew you were right. Armed with a pair of 2½-foot shortees and a pair of four-foot ones, I flew to my favorite ski resort in Austria. Results were instantaneous.

"On my own, after two days on the 2½-footers, I mastered linked parallel turns. I could turn when and where I wanted. A couple of days on the four-footers, and I skied with security and precision.

"I can only compare the feeling with the exultation of flying.

"At the end of two weeks' skiing, I entered the open slalom race sponsored by the local ski school. I zipped through all the gates perfectly parallel and placed fourth in a field of 34. They gave me a prize for 'best form.'

"Short skis have opened up a new world for me at a time in life when new worlds are hard to come by."

All through this book the emphasis has been on parallel turning technique for a very good reason. It is the easiest and safest way to ski in control.

If you practice the three basic turns (foot-turn, leg-turn, hip-turn) consistently, you will find yourself in control of your skis on any slope in any snow. You'll be a good skier all your life.